CHOOSE TO BELIEVE IN MIRACLES.

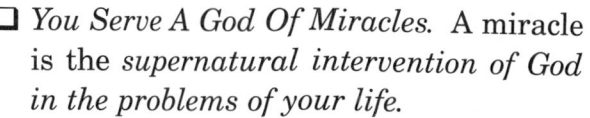

- *You Serve A God Of Miracles.* A miracle is the *supernatural intervention of God in the problems of your life.*

- By believing in the Power of God, you have nothing to lose and everything to gain.

- At *some point* in your life, you will either be forced to live in the *potential of your faith*, or with the *consequences of your doubt*.

The Word

"Jesus said unto him, If thou canst believe, all things are possible to him that believeth." (Mk. 9:23)

≈ 2 ≈

NEVER DOUBT THE LOVE OF GOD.

❏ *The World's Greatest Miracle Happened 2000 Years Ago.* God gave His Son Jesus to die on the cross for our sins. *Calvary was a miracle.*

❏ His mercy and forgiveness are *proof* that He cares. Your life, your health and your happiness matter.

❏ The same God who removes the *stain* of sin from your *heart*, also removes sickness, disease and poverty from your life. His *love* should make it easier for you to expect your miracle today.

The Word

"For God so loved the world, that He gave His only begotten Son, that whosoever believeth in Him should not perish, but have everlasting life."

(Jn. 3:16)

3

RESPECT THE LAW OF AGREEMENT.

❑ Satan Fears *Relationship*. He made no attempt to destroy Adam until Eve entered his life. *Two are better than one.*

❑ God celebrates *unity*. He honors agreement regarding your miracle.

❑ Be *quick to recognize* a God-sent prayer partner.

The Word

"Verily I say unto you, Whatsoever ye shall bind on earth shall be bound in heaven: and whatsoever ye shall loose on earth shall be loosed in heaven. Again I say unto you, That if two of you shall agree on earth as touching any thing that they shall ask, it shall be done for them of My Father which is in heaven." (Matt. 18:18,19)

4

CONFESS AND FORSAKE ANY KNOWN SIN.

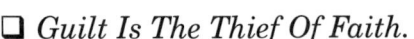

- *Guilt Is The Thief Of Faith.*

- When you permit sin in your life, you become *uncomfortable* in the presence of God.

- It is difficult to expect a miracle from a God you resent. *Confess your failure.* He forgives.

The Word
"If I regard iniquity in my heart, the Lord will not hear me:" (Ps. 66:18)

≈ 5 ≈

PURSUE YOUR MIRACLE.

❑ Pursuit Is The *Proof* Of Desire. When you really want something, you are willing to *reach* for it.

❑ Miracles happen *only* to those who *seek* them.

❑ The blind man *cried* out to Jesus. The hemorrhaging woman *pressed* through the crowd to touch His garment. You too, must be *willing* to put forth an *effort*. Use your Faith to get what you want from God.

=== *The Word* ===
"Ask, and it shall be given you; seek, and ye shall find; knock, and it shall be opened unto you: For every one that asketh receiveth; and he that seeketh findeth; and to him that knocketh it shall be opened." (Matt. 7:7,8)

6

FOCUS YOUR FAITH.

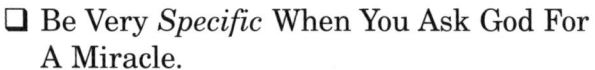

- ❑ Be Very *Specific* When You Ask God For A Miracle.

- ❑ Be exact in your request for a specific salary increase or business opportunity. Don't simply ask for "more" finances.

- ❑ Focus on the particular need you want God to meet. Don't let anyone's attitude or words distract you.

The Word

"Or what man is there of you, whom if his son ask bread, will he give him a stone? Or if he ask a fish, will he give him a serpent? If ye then, being evil, know how to give good gifts unto your children, how much more shall your Father which is in heaven give good things to them that ask Him?"

(Matt. 7:9-11)

7

HOLD OUT FOR THE BEST.

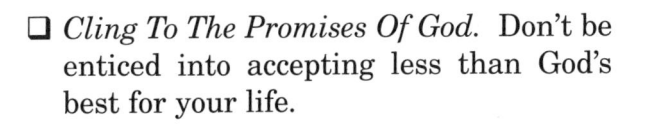

❑ *Cling To The Promises Of God.* Don't be enticed into accepting less than God's best for your life.

❑ Substitutions are common satanic ploys. Jesus was proof that God cared enough to send His *best*.

❑ Your faith cannot respond to two targets. So, never consider any alternative to your miracle.

The Word

"But let him ask in faith, nothing wavering. For he that wavereth is like a wave of the sea driven with the wind and tossed. For let not that man think that he shall receive any thing of the Lord. A double minded man is unstable in all his ways." (James 1:6-8)

8

DISCARD YOUR DOUBTS.

- Miracles Happen Only To The *Believing*. So *believe*.

- Doubts never produce your desired results.

- Stop advertising your doubts. Start *celebrating your expectations* of a miracle.

The Word
"Verily I say unto you, If ye have faith, and doubt not, ye shall not only do this which is done to the fig tree, but also if ye shall say unto this mountain, Be thou removed, and be thou cast into the sea; it shall be done." (Matt. 21:21)

9

SPEAK TO YOUR MOUNTAIN.

❏ *Your Mountain Is Any Problem That You Are Facing.* Address it with authority and command it to move in the name of Jesus.

❏ Every mountain is a *servant* to your Faith. It *must* obey. Few have mastered the art of verbally *commanding* their mountains to *move*.

❏ Losers talk *about* their mountain ...Champions talk *to* their mountain.

The Word

"That whosoever shall say unto this mountain, Be thou removed, and be thou cast into the sea; and shall not doubt in his heart, but shall believe that those things which he saith shall come to pass; he shall have whatsoever he saith."

(Mk. 11:23)

10

ACCEPT THE UNEXPLAINABLE.

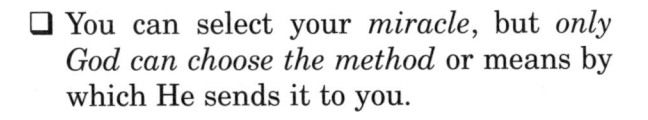

- ❏ You can select your *miracle*, but *only God can choose the method* or means by which He sends it to you.

- ❏ Jesus used clay and spittle in the healing of the blind man...filling up water pots to create wine at the marriage of Cana. His methods are puzzling, unpredictable and always illogical to the natural mind of man.

- ❏ Those who argue over the *methods* of God rarely receive the *Miracles of God*.

The Word

"For My thoughts are not your thoughts, neither are your ways My ways, saith the Lord. For as the heavens are higher than the earth, so are My ways higher than your ways, and My thoughts than your thoughts." (Isa. 55:8,9)

~ 11 ~

EXPECT A TURN-AROUND.

❏ Today Is Not *Permanent*. Your worst circumstances today are subject to *change*.

❏ God is stepping into the Arena of your life. He is turning the tide in your favor.

❏ *You Are Never As Far From A Miracle As It First Appears.*

The Word
"Every valley shall be exalted, and every mountain and hill shall be made low: and the crooked shall be made straight, and the rough places plain: And the glory of the Lord shall be revealed, and all flesh shall see it together: for the mouth of the Lord hath spoken it."

(Isa. 40:4,5)

12

PRACTICE FAITH-TALK.

- *Your Words Are Deciding Tomorrow.*

- Every word you speak today will paint a portrait of Faith, both in your mind and the minds of those around you.

- Today, season *every conversation* with *Faith-Talk*. Tell everyone what you are expecting God to do in *your* life.

The Word

"Finally, brethren, whatsoever things are true, whatsoever things are honest, whatsoever things are just, whatsoever things are pure, whatsoever things are lovely, whatsoever things are of good report; if there be any virtue, and if there be any praise, think on these things." (Phil. 4:8)

≈ 13 ≈

CELEBRATE THE HEALER.

- *Sickness Comes From Satan.* Jesus came to *destroy* the works of the devil.

- God really wants you to be well, healthy and whole. Jesus has *already paid the price* through the stripes He bore on Calvary.

- *Celebrate* His healing presence through you right now.

The Word
"How God anointed Jesus of Nazareth with the Holy Ghost and with power: Who went about doing good, and healing all that were oppressed of the devil; for God was with Him." (Acts 10:38)

～ 14 ～

MAKE UP YOUR MIND TO BE HEALED.

❑ *Whatever You Can Tolerate, You Cannot Change.*

❑ *Become tenacious.* Resist sickness. Cling to the Healer.

❑ Your persistence will *demoralize* satan and *attract the attention of God.*

❑ *Demons dread a fighter.*

═══════ ***The Word*** ═══════
"And, behold, a woman, which was diseased with an issue of blood twelve years, came behind Him, and touched the hem of His garment: For she said within herself, If I may but touch His garment, I shall be whole."

(Matt. 9:20,21)

~ 15 ~

Don't Limit God.

❑ You Are The *Creation*. He is your *Creator*. You cannot *out-think* the One Who made you.

❑ He delights in performing the Impossible. He turns sickness into health...poverty into prosperity...tears into laughter.

❑ He is the Master of the Turnaround. Don't underestimate Him.

The Word
"With men it is impossible, but not with God: for with God all things are possible." (Mk. 10:27)

16

BIND AND RESTRAIN SATANIC ATTACKS.

- *You Are A Child Of God.* You carry His authority on earth. *Satan is subject to you.*

- He must yield to the *knowledgeable* believer.

- Declare aloud now, "Satan, take your hands off my home, my family, my health, my finances, in Jesus' name."

The Word
"Whatsoever ye shall bind on earth shall be bound in heaven: and whatsoever ye shall loose on earth shall be loosed in heaven." (Matt. 18:18)

17

RECEIVE MINISTERS WHO TEACH MIRACLES.

- When Men Of God Talk...*Listen.* Ministers are gifts of God to the Church.

- When God talks to the Body of Christ, He speaks through men and women.

- If you want your Faith to grow—you must be willing to be *taught* and *mentored* by those who carry God's special anointing for healing and miracles.

The Word

"And He gave some, apostles; and some, prophets; and some, evangelists; and some, pastors and teachers; For the perfecting of the saints, for the work of the ministry, for the edifying of the body of Christ:" (Eph. 4:11,12)

18

CREATE A MIRACLE-CLIMATE.

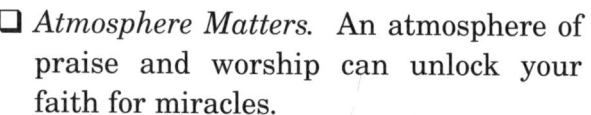

- *Atmosphere Matters.* An atmosphere of praise and worship can unlock your faith for miracles.

- When David played his harp for Saul, evil spirits *departed* from the palace. *Anointed* music is one of the Master Keys in creating a Miracle-Climate.

- Keep a cassette player handy. *Use it* to make a conscious effort today to keep Godly music playing all day long.

The Word

"But now bring me a minstrel. And it came to pass, when the minstrel played, that the hand of the Lord came upon him." (2 Kings 3:15)

19

FEED YOUR FAITH DAILY.

- *Faith Is Your Confidence In God.* Sometimes it is weak or may even seem nonexistent. At other times, it may be powerful and incredibly strong. It depends on the food you feed it.

- Faith is a *Tool*...a *Key*...a *Weapon*. A Tool to create a future; a Key to unlock God's Storehouse of Blessing; and the Weapon that defeats satan.

- *Faith Comes When You Hear God Talk.* Listen today to His Spirit, His Servants, His Scriptures.

The Word
"So then faith cometh by hearing, and hearing by the word of God."

(Rom. 10:17)

20

DARE TO DREAM AGAIN.

❑ *Wake Up The Dreamer Within You.*

❑ Stop Looking At Where You Have *Been* And Start Looking At *Where You Are Going.* Tomorrow is not here yet. *Birth it.*

❑ God is a God of the Second-Chance. He is a God of Miracles. *He has never changed His plans for your life.* Seasons change, but God's promises to you have not. Your miracle is just ahead.

The Word

"The glory of this latter house shall be greater than of the former, saith the Lord of hosts: and in this place will I give peace, saith the Lord of hosts."

(Hag. 2:9)

21

PREPARE FOR MIRACLES TODAY.

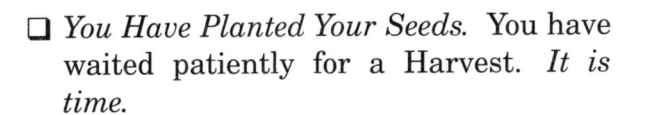

- *You Have Planted Your Seeds.* You have waited patiently for a Harvest. *It is time.*

- *Delay is not denial.* Like an unborn child in a mother's womb, you have been carrying the Seed of your miracle within you. Faithfully. *Expectantly.*

- *God always keeps His appointments.* Expect something incredible to happen *today.*

The Word
"For the vision is yet for an appointed time, but at the end it shall speak, and not lie: though it tarry, wait for it: because it will surely come, it will not tarry." (Hab. 2:3)

22

HONOR A POINT-OF-CONTACT.

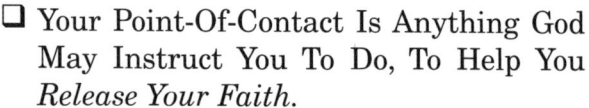

- Your Point-Of-Contact Is Anything God May Instruct You To Do, To Help You *Release Your Faith.*

- The Israelites obeyed God's command to *walk* around the walls of Jericho. The widow of Zarephath *planted her food* as a Seed into the ministry of Elijah. *Your point-of-contact is any act of obedience that proves your faith in God.*

- It is unexplainable, yet powerful. So, simply do *whatever God tells you to do today.*

=== ***The Word*** ===
"His mother saith unto the servants, Whatsoever He saith unto you, do it."
(Jn. 2:5)

≈ 23 ≈

EXPECT YOUR MIRACLE.

❑ *Expectation Is Acting As If Your Miracle Has Already Happened.*

❑ Organize your life around your expected miracle. Plan it. Talk it. *Believe it.*

❑ *Expectation qualifies you for receivership.* It separates you. It transfers you from the masses who *need* miracles...to the chosen who *receive* them.

The Word
"But without faith it is impossible to please Him: for he that cometh to God must believe that He is, and that He is a rewarder of them that diligently seek Him." (Heb. 11:6)

~ 24 ~
DECIDE TO RECEIVE.

❏ Your Seed Is *Anything You Plant To Create A Desired Result Or Harvest.*

❏ Your Harvest is *any benefit or blessing you have decided to receive from God.*

❏ Your *Source* is Jehovah-Jireh, the God who provides. He is unlimited, impartial and generous.

~ 25 ~
TALK TOTAL PROSPERITY.

❏ *You Are The Offspring Of A Perfect God. Talk* like it.

❏ His covenant with you is forever. *Think* like it.

❏ His prosperity is penetrating every area of your life. *Live* like it.

The Word
"But my God shall supply all your need according to His riches in glory by Christ Jesus." (Phil. 4:19)

≈ 26 ≈

GET EXCITED ABOUT FEELING GOOD.

- Sickness Is A *Thief.* It steals *time* from those you love. It steals *money* that could be used to achieve your goals. It steals *energy* necessary to complete God's plans in your life.

- God wants you *well.* Get excited over it. The Great Physician is putting you back together.

- *Decide* to be healthy. *Decide* to feel good. *Decide* to be well.

The Word

"Surely He hath borne our griefs, and carried our sorrows: yet we did esteem Him stricken, smitten of God, and afflicted. But He was wounded for our transgressions, He was bruised for our iniquities: the chastisement of our peace was upon Him; and with His stripes we are healed." (Isa. 53:4,5)

~ 27 ~

VISUALIZE YOUR MIRACLE.

❑ *God Begins Every Miracle With A Mind-Photograph.* This is normal. Every architect draws a picture before the building begins.

❑ Abraham visualized his generations of children every time he beheld the stars at night.

❑ Use your *memory. Replay* past victories. Use your *imagination* to *pre-play* in your mind those miracles that your heart has desired from the Lord. David did this and defeated the giant, Goliath.

The Word

"And He brought him forth abroad, and said, Look now toward heaven, and tell the stars, if thou be able to number them: and He said unto him, So shall thy seed be." (Gen. 15:5)

≈ 28 ≈
NEVER QUIT REACHING.

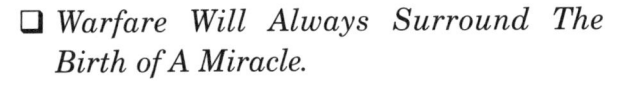

- *Warfare Will Always Surround The Birth of A Miracle.*

- Champions make the extra effort to *try one more time.*

- Miracles are not for the holy, they are for the *hungry.* The grapes of God's blessings are not placed within your mouth, but *within your reach. Don't quit* until you get what you want from God.

The Word
"The Lord is good unto them that wait for Him, to the soul that seeketh Him."
(Lam. 3:25)

29

TARGET YOUR SEED-FAITH.

- *Your Tithes And Offerings Are Seeds That You Sow.* Seed-Faith is sowing what you have been *given* to create something you have been *promised*.

- Elijah taught the Seed-Faith principle to the widow of Zarephath. She believed it. She planted a portion of what she had back into the work of God. She expected her "Seed" to be multiplied back to her. It happened.

- Plant a Seed today into the work of God. *Wrap* your Faith around it and remember that the Seed that leaves your hand *really never leaves your life.* It goes into your *future* where it *multiplies*.

The Word

"Bring ye all the tithes into the storehouse, that there may be meat in Mine house, and prove Me now herewith, saith the Lord of hosts, if I will not open you the windows of heaven, and pour you out a blessing, that there shall not be room enough to receive it." (Mal. 3:10)

~ 30 ~
PRAY FOR SOMEONE ELSE.

- ❏ One of the Master Keys to personal miracles is to *get involved with the needs of others.*

- ❏ Joseph used his gift of interpreting dreams to calm a tormented Pharaoh. He was promoted from the prison to the palace. Job prayed for his friends during the worst crisis of his life. It released God to *reverse the curse.*

- ❏ God's contribution to *you* is always determined by what you have chosen to contribute to *others*. *What You Make Happen For Others, God Will Make Happen For You* (Eph. 6:8).

The Word
"And the Lord turned the captivity of Job, when he prayed for his friends: also the Lord gave Job twice as much as he had before." (Job 42:10)

~ 31 ~

PROMOTE THE POWER OF JESUS.

❑ The first two letters of the word "gospel" spell..."Go."

❑ Christianity is a network of activity. Promote Jesus today. He is the Starting-Point of every miracle. Be the bridge that connects Him to somebody in trouble today.

❑ Be bold. *One Miracle Is Worth A Thousand Sermons.*

=== *The Word* ===

"Go ye into all the world, and preach the gospel to every creature. And these signs shall follow them that believe; In My name shall they cast out devils; they shall speak with new tongues; They shall take up serpents; and if they drink any deadly thing, it shall not hurt them; they shall lay hands on the sick, and they shall recover." (Mk. 16:15,17,18)

ABOUT *MIKE MURDOCK*

- Has embraced his Assignment to pursue...possess...and publish the Wisdom of God to help people achieve their dreams and goals.

- Began full-time evangelism at the age of 19, which has continued since 1966.

- Has traveled and spoken to more than 14,000 audiences in 38 countries, including East and West Africa, the Orient, and Europe.

- Noted author of 130 books, including best sellers, *"Wisdom For Winning," "Dream Seeds"* and *"The Double Diamond Principle."*

- Created the popular *"Topical Bible"* series for Businessmen, Mothers, Fathers, Teenagers, and the *"One-Minute Pocket Bible"* series and *"The Uncommon Life"* series.

- Has composed more than 5,700 songs such as *"I Am Blessed," "You Can Make It," "Holy Spirit This Is Your House"* and *"Jesus, Just The Mention Of Your Name,"* recorded by many gospel artists.

- Is the Founder of The Wisdom Center, in Denton Texas.

- Has a weekly television program called *"Wisdom Keys With Mike Murdock."*

- Has appeared often on TBN, CBN, and other television network programs.

- Is a Founding Trustee on the Board of Charismatic Bible Ministries with Oral Roberts.

- Has had more than 3,500 accept the call into full-time ministry under his ministry.

DECISION PAGE

Will You Accept Jesus As Your Personal Savior Today?

The Bible says, "That if thou shalt confess with thy mouth the Lord Jesus, and shalt believe in thine heart that God hath raised Him from the dead, thou shalt be saved" (Rom. 10:9).

Pray this prayer from your heart today!

"Dear Jesus, I believe that You died for me and rose again on the third day. I confess I am a sinner...I need Your love and forgiveness...Come into my heart. Forgive my sins. I receive Your eternal life. Confirm Your love by giving me peace, joy and supernatural love for others. Amen."

Return this today!

☐ Yes, Mike! I made a decision to accept Christ as my personal Savior today. Please send me my free gift of your book, *"31 Keys To A New Beginning"* to help me with my new life in Christ. *(B-48)*

NAME		BIRTHDAY
ADDRESS		
CITY	STATE	ZIP
PHONE	E-MAIL	*B-15*

Mail Form To:
The Wisdom Center · P. O. Box 99 · Denton, TX 76202
1-888-WISDOM-1 (1-888-947-3661)
Website: ***www.thewisdomcenter.cc***

(Clip and Mail)

Unless otherwise indicated, all Scripture quotations are taken from the King James Version of the Bible.
Seeds Of Wisdom On Miracles · ISBN 1-56394-082-5
Copyright © 2001 by *MIKE MURDOCK*
All publishing rights belong exclusively to Wisdom International
Published by The Wisdom Center · P.O. Box 99 · Denton, TX 76202
1-888-WISDOM-1 (1-888-947-3661) · Website:www.thewisdomcenter.cc
Printed in the United States of America. All rights reserved under International Copyright Law. Contents and/or cover may not be reproduced in whole or in part in any form without the express written consent of the publisher.

WISDOM 12 PAK

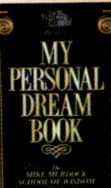 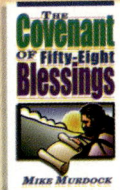 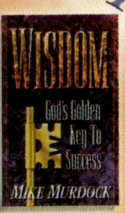

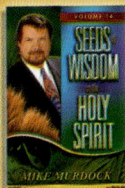    

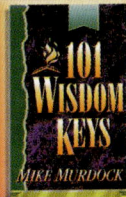  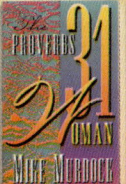 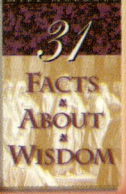

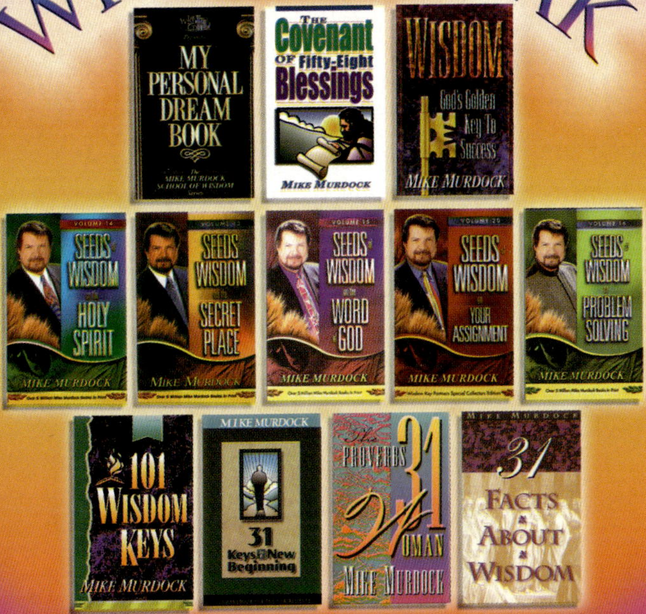

1. MY PERSONAL DREAM BOOK - B143 - $5.00
2. THE COVENANT OF FIFTY-EIGHT BLESSINGS - B47 - $8.00
3. WISDOM, GOD'S GOLDEN KEY TO SUCCESS - B71 - $7.00
4. SEEDS OF WISDOM ON THE HOLY SPIRIT - B116 - $5.00
5. SEEDS OF WISDOM ON THE SECRET PLACE - B115 - $5.00
6. SEEDS OF WISDOM ON THE WORD OF GOD - B117 - $5.00
7. SEEDS OF WISDOM ON YOUR ASSIGNMENT - B122 - $5.00
8. SEEDS OF WISDOM ON PROBLEM SOLVING - B118 - $5.00
9. 101 WISDOM KEYS - B45 - $7.00
10. 31 KEYS TO A NEW BEGINNING - B48 - $7.00
11. THE PROVERBS 31 WOMAN - B49 - $7.00
12. 31 FACTS ABOUT WISDOM - B46 - $7.00

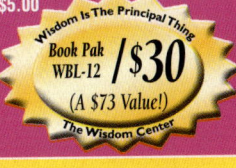

Wisdom Is The Principal Thing
Book Pak WBL-12 / $30
(A $73 Value!)
The Wisdom Center

ORDER TODAY! 1-888-WISDOM-1
www.thewisdomcenter.cc (1-888-947-3661)

THE WISDOM CENTER • P.O. Box 99 • Denton, TX 76202

Money Matters.

This Powerful Video will unleash the Financial Harvest of your lifetime!

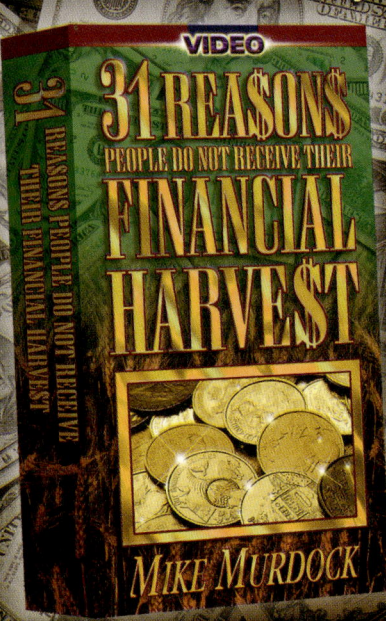

- 8 Scriptural Reasons You Should Pursue Financial Prosperity
- The Secret Prayer Key You Need When Making A Financial Request To God
- The Weapon Of Expectation And The 5 Miracles It Unlocks
- How To Discern Those Who Qualify To Receive Your Financial Assistance
- How To Predict The Miracle Moment God Will Schedule Your Financial Breakthrough

Wisdom Is The Principal Thing
Video VI-17 / $30
Six Audio Tapes / $30 TS-71
Book / $12 B-82
The Wisdom Center

ORDER TODAY! 1-888-WISDOM-1
www.thewisdomcenter.cc (1-888-947-3661)

THE WISDOM CENTER • P.O. Box 99 • Denton, TX 76202

The Secret To 1000 Times More.

In this Dynamic Video you will find answers to unleash Financial Flow into your life!

- Habits Of Uncommon Achievers
- The Greatest Success Law I Ever Discovered
- How To Discern Your Place Of Assignment, The Only Place Financial Provision Is Guaranteed
- 3 Secret Keys In Solving Problems For Others
- How To Become The Next Person To Receive A Raise On Your Job

Wisdom Is The Principal Thing
Video VI-16 / $30
Six Audio Tapes / $30 TS-104
Book / $10 B-104
The Wisdom Center

ORDER TODAY! 1-888-WISDOM-1
www.thewisdomcenter.cc (1-888-947-3661)

THE WISDOM CENTER • P.O. Box 99 • Denton, TX 76202

Somebody's Future Will Not Begin Until You Enter.

THIS COLLECTION INCLUDES 4 DIFFERENT BOOKS CONTAINING UNCOMMON WISDOM FOR DISCOVERING YOUR LIFE ASSIGNMENT

- How To Achieve A God-Given Dream And Goal
- How To Know Who Is Assigned To You
- The Purpose And Rewards Of An Enemy

Wisdom Is The Principal Thing
Book Pak WBL-14 / $30
Buy 3-Get 1 Free
($10 Each/$40 Value!)
The Wisdom Center

ORDER TODAY! 1-888-WISDOM-1
www.thewisdomcenter.cc (1-888-947-3661)

THE WISDOM CENTER • P.O. Box 99 • Denton, TX 76202

THE SECRET.

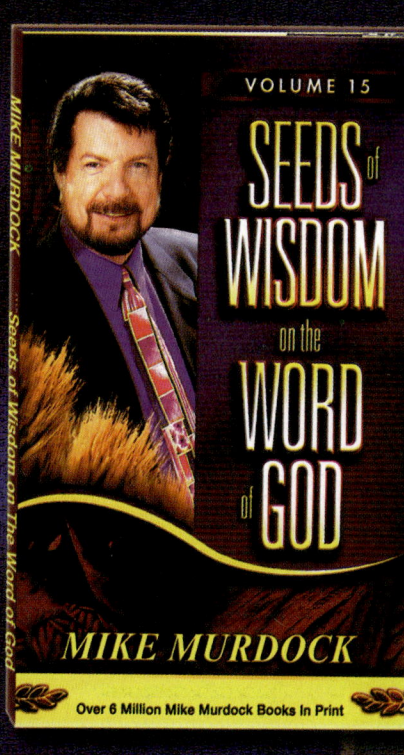

- 11 Reasons Why The Bible Is The Most Important Book On Earth
- 12 Problems The Word Of God Can Solve In Your Life
- 4 Of My Personal Bible Reading Secrets
- 4 Steps To Building A Spiritual Home
- 9 Wisdom Keys To Being Successful In Developing The Habit Of Reading The Word Of God

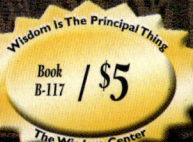

Book B-117 / $5

ORDER TODAY! 1-888-WISDOM-1
www.thewisdomcenter.cc (1-888-947-3661)

THE WISDOM CENTER • P.O. Box 99 • Denton, TX 76202

WISDOM COLLECTION

SECRETS OF THE UNCOMMON MILLIONAIRE

1. The Uncommon Millionaire Conference Vol. 1 (Six Cassettes)
2. The Uncommon Millionaire Conference Vol. 2 (Six Cassettes)
3. The Uncommon Millionaire Conference Vol. 3 (Six Cassettes)
4. The Uncommon Millionaire Conference Vol. 4 (Six Cassettes)
5. 31 Reasons People Do Not Receive Their Financial Harvest (256 Page Book)
6. Secrets of the Richest Man Who Ever Lived (178 Page Book)
7. 12 Seeds Of Wisdom Books On 12 Topics
8. The Gift Of Wisdom For Leaders Desk Calendar
9. 101 Wisdom Keys On Tape (Audio Tape)
10. In Honor Of The Holy Spirit (Music Cassette)
11. 365 Memorization Scriptures On The Word Of God (Audio Cassette)

Wisdom Is The Principal Thing
THE WISDOM COLLECTION 8
SECRETS OF THE UNCOMMON MILLIONAIRE
WC-08 / $195
The Wisdom Center

ORDER TODAY! 1-888-WISDOM-1
www.thewisdomcenter.cc (1-888-947-3661)

THE WISDOM CENTER • P.O. Box 99 • Denton, TX 76202

The Secrets For Surviving.

- How To Get Through The Storms Of Your Life!
- Avoiding the #1 Trap Satan Uses Against Believers!
- Keys To Discovering Wrong People In Your Life!
- Satan's 3 Most Effective Weapons!
- How To Use Adversity As A Stepping Stone To Wisdom!
- How To Stand When Everything Is Falling Apart!
- Six Seasons Satan Always Attacks You!
- Battle Techniques Of War-Weary Saints!
- Reversing Satanic Strategy!
- How To Get Back Up When The Devil Puts You Down

Six Wisdom Cassettes That Will Multiply Your Success!

Wisdom Is The Principal Thing
Tape Pak TS-18 / $30
Six Audio Tapes
The Wisdom Center

This life changing and revolutionary teaching is based on the Wisdom and The Principles of other champions in the Word of God. You will discover the greatest Wisdom Keys on earth and will begin unlocking the treasure containing every desired gift and miracle you are pursuing.

ORDER TODAY! 1-888-WISDOM-1
(1-888-947-3661)
www.thewisdomcenter.cc

THE WISDOM CENTER • P.O. Box 99 • Denton, TX 76202